LOG BOOK

I0392755

Log Book No._____

Continued From Log Book No. _____ Continued to Log Book No._____

Assigned To:

Name_____

Signature_____ Date_____

Date Issued_____ By_____

Phone_____ Email_____

Company / University / College _____

Department_____

Address_____
_____

City_____ State_____ Zip_____

Date Log Book Completed_____

Number of Pages Filled In_____

Notes:

BALANCE CALIBRATION LOG BOOK

Reference: **ID Number:**

Date	Initials	Calibration Weight	Actual Weight	Control Parameters	Maintenance and Adjustments
Signature			Date		Title
Witness			Date		Title

BALANCE CALIBRATION LOG BOOK

Reference: ID Number:

Date	Initials	Calibration Weight	Actual Weight	Control Parameters	Maintenance and Adjustments
Signature			Date		Title
Witness			Date		Title

BALANCE CALIBRATION LOG BOOK

Reference: **ID Number:**

Date	Initials	Calibration Weight	Actual Weight	Control Parameters	Maintenance and Adjustments

| Signature | | Date | | Title | |
| Witness | | Date | | Title | |

BALANCE CALIBRATION LOG BOOK

Reference: **ID Number:**

Date	Initials	Calibration Weight	Actual Weight	Control Parameters	Maintenance and Adjustments

Signature			Date		Title
Witness			Date		Title

BALANCE CALIBRATION LOG BOOK

Reference: **ID Number:**

Date	Initials	Calibration Weight	Actual Weight	Control Parameters	Maintenance and Adjustments
Signature			Date		Title
Witness			Date		Title

BALANCE CALIBRATION LOG BOOK

Reference: ID Number:

Date	Initials	Calibration Weight	Actual Weight	Control Parameters	Maintenance and Adjustments
Signature			Date		Title
Witness			Date		Title

BALANCE CALIBRATION LOG BOOK

Reference: **ID Number:**

Date	Initials	Calibration Weight	Actual Weight	Control Parameters	Maintenance and Adjustments

| Signature | | Date | | Title | |
| Witness | | Date | | Title | |

BALANCE CALIBRATION LOG BOOK

Reference: ID Number:

Date	Initials	Calibration Weight	Actual Weight	Control Parameters	Maintenance and Adjustments

| Signature | | | Date | | Title |
| Witness | | | Date | | Title |

BALANCE CALIBRATION LOG BOOK

Reference: ID Number:

Date	Initials	Calibration Weight	Actual Weight	Control Parameters	Maintenance and Adjustments

| Signature | | Date | | Title | |
| Witness | | Date | | Title | |

BALANCE CALIBRATION LOG BOOK

Reference: **ID Number:**

Date	Initials	Calibration Weight	Actual Weight	Control Parameters	Maintenance and Adjustments
Signature			Date		Title
Witness			Date		Title

BALANCE CALIBRATION LOG BOOK

Reference: ID Number:

Date	Initials	Calibration Weight	Actual Weight	Control Parameters	Maintenance and Adjustments

| Signature | | Date | | Title | |
| Witness | | Date | | Title | |

BALANCE CALIBRATION LOG BOOK

Reference: **ID Number:**

Date	Initials	Calibration Weight	Actual Weight	Control Parameters	Maintenance and Adjustments
Signature			Date		Title
Witness			Date		Title

BALANCE CALIBRATION LOG BOOK

Reference: **ID Number:**

Date	Initials	Calibration Weight	Actual Weight	Control Parameters	Maintenance and Adjustments
Signature			Date		Title
Witness			Date		Title

BALANCE CALIBRATION LOG BOOK

Reference: ID Number:

Date	Initials	Calibration Weight	Actual Weight	Control Parameters	Maintenance and Adjustments
Signature			Date		Title
Witness			Date		Title

BALANCE CALIBRATION LOG BOOK

Reference: ID Number:

Date	Initials	Calibration Weight	Actual Weight	Control Parameters	Maintenance and Adjustments
Signature			Date		Title
Witness			Date		Title

BALANCE CALIBRATION LOG BOOK

Reference: **ID Number:**

Date	Initials	Calibration Weight	Actual Weight	Control Parameters	Maintenance and Adjustments
Signature			Date		Title
Witness			Date		Title

BALANCE CALIBRATION LOG BOOK

Reference: **ID Number:**

Date	Initials	Calibration Weight	Actual Weight	Control Parameters	Maintenance and Adjustments
Signature			Date		Title
Witness			Date		Title

BALANCE CALIBRATION LOG BOOK

Reference: **ID Number:**

Date	Initials	Calibration Weight	Actual Weight	Control Parameters	Maintenance and Adjustments
Signature			Date		Title
Witness			Date		Title

BALANCE CALIBRATION LOG BOOK

Reference: ID Number:

Date	Initials	Calibration Weight	Actual Weight	Control Parameters	Maintenance and Adjustments
Signature				Date		Title
Witness				Date		Title

BALANCE CALIBRATION LOG BOOK

Reference: **ID Number:**

Date	Initials	Calibration Weight	Actual Weight	Control Parameters	Maintenance and Adjustments

| Signature | | | Date | | Title |
| Witness | | | Date | | Title |

BALANCE CALIBRATION LOG BOOK

Reference: **ID Number:**

Date	Initials	Calibration Weight	Actual Weight	Control Parameters	Maintenance and Adjustments
Signature			Date		Title
Witness			Date		Title

BALANCE CALIBRATION LOG BOOK

Reference: ID Number:

Date	Initials	Calibration Weight	Actual Weight	Control Parameters	Maintenance and Adjustments
Signature			Date		Title
Witness			Date		Title

BALANCE CALIBRATION LOG BOOK

Reference: ID Number:

Date	Initials	Calibration Weight	Actual Weight	Control Parameters	Maintenance and Adjustments

| Signature | | Date | | Title | |
| Witness | | Date | | Title | |

BALANCE CALIBRATION LOG BOOK

Reference: **ID Number:**

Date	Initials	Calibration Weight	Actual Weight	Control Parameters	Maintenance and Adjustments
Signature			Date		Title
Witness			Date		Title

BALANCE CALIBRATION LOG BOOK

Reference: ID Number:

Date	Initials	Calibration Weight	Actual Weight	Control Parameters	Maintenance and Adjustments
Signature			Date		Title
Witness			Date		Title

BALANCE CALIBRATION LOG BOOK

Reference: ID Number:

Date	Initials	Calibration Weight	Actual Weight	Control Parameters	Maintenance and Adjustments
Signature			Date		Title
Witness			Date		Title

BALANCE CALIBRATION LOG BOOK

Reference: **ID Number:**

Date	Initials	Calibration Weight	Actual Weight	Control Parameters	Maintenance and Adjustments
Signature			Date		Title
Witness			Date		Title

BALANCE CALIBRATION LOG BOOK

Reference: **ID Number:**

Date	Initials	Calibration Weight	Actual Weight	Control Parameters	Maintenance and Adjustments

Signature	Date	Title
Witness	Date	Title

BALANCE CALIBRATION LOG BOOK

Reference: ID Number:

Date	Initials	Calibration Weight	Actual Weight	Control Parameters	Maintenance and Adjustments
Signature			Date		Title
Witness			Date		Title

BALANCE CALIBRATION LOG BOOK

Reference: ID Number:

Date	Initials	Calibration Weight	Actual Weight	Control Parameters	Maintenance and Adjustments
Signature			Date		Title
Witness			Date		Title

BALANCE CALIBRATION LOG BOOK

Reference: ID Number:

Date	Initials	Calibration Weight	Actual Weight	Control Parameters	Maintenance and Adjustments
Signature			Date		Title
Witness			Date		Title

BALANCE CALIBRATION LOG BOOK

Reference: **ID Number:**

Date	Initials	Calibration Weight	Actual Weight	Control Parameters	Maintenance and Adjustments
Signature			Date		Title
Witness			Date		Title

BALANCE CALIBRATION LOG BOOK

Reference:					ID Number:

Date	Initials	Calibration Weight	Actual Weight	Control Parameters	Maintenance and Adjustments
Signature			Date		Title
Witness			Date		Title

BALANCE CALIBRATION LOG BOOK

Reference: **ID Number:**

Date	Initials	Calibration Weight	Actual Weight	Control Parameters	Maintenance and Adjustments
Signature			Date		Title
Witness			Date		Title

BALANCE CALIBRATION LOG BOOK

Reference: ID Number:

Date	Initials	Calibration Weight	Actual Weight	Control Parameters	Maintenance and Adjustments
Signature			Date		Title
Witness			Date		Title

BALANCE CALIBRATION LOG BOOK

Reference: **ID Number:**

Date	Initials	Calibration Weight	Actual Weight	Control Parameters	Maintenance and Adjustments
Signature				Date	Title
Witness				Date	Title

BALANCE CALIBRATION LOG BOOK

Reference: ID Number:

Date	Initials	Calibration Weight	Actual Weight	Control Parameters	Maintenance and Adjustments
Signature			Date		Title
Witness			Date		Title

BALANCE CALIBRATION LOG BOOK

Reference:	ID Number:

Date	Initials	Calibration Weight	Actual Weight	Control Parameters	Maintenance and Adjustments
Signature			Date		Title
Witness			Date		Title

BALANCE CALIBRATION LOG BOOK

Reference: ID Number:

Date	Initials	Calibration Weight	Actual Weight	Control Parameters	Maintenance and Adjustments
Signature			Date		Title
Witness			Date		Title

BALANCE CALIBRATION LOG BOOK

Reference: **ID Number:**

Date	Initials	Calibration Weight	Actual Weight	Control Parameters	Maintenance and Adjustments
Signature			Date		Title
Witness			Date		Title

BALANCE CALIBRATION LOG BOOK

Reference: **ID Number:**

Date	Initials	Calibration Weight	Actual Weight	Control Parameters	Maintenance and Adjustments
Signature			Date		Title
Witness			Date		Title

BALANCE CALIBRATION LOG BOOK

Reference: ID Number:

Date	Initials	Calibration Weight	Actual Weight	Control Parameters	Maintenance and Adjustments

Signature		Date	Title
Witness		Date	Title

BALANCE CALIBRATION LOG BOOK

Reference:　　　　　　　　　　　　ID Number:

Date	Initials	Calibration Weight	Actual Weight	Control Parameters	Maintenance and Adjustments

Signature		Date		Title	
Witness		Date		Title	

BALANCE CALIBRATION LOG BOOK

Reference:				ID Number:	
Date	Initials	Calibration Weight	Actual Weight	Control Parameters	Maintenance and Adjustments
Signature			Date		Title
Witness			Date		Title

BALANCE CALIBRATION LOG BOOK

Reference: **ID Number:**

Date	Initials	Calibration Weight	Actual Weight	Control Parameters	Maintenance and Adjustments
Signature			Date		Title
Witness			Date		Title

BALANCE CALIBRATION LOG BOOK

Reference: ID Number:

Date	Initials	Calibration Weight	Actual Weight	Control Parameters	Maintenance and Adjustments
Signature			Date		Title
Witness			Date		Title

BALANCE CALIBRATION LOG BOOK

Reference: **ID Number:**

Date	Initials	Calibration Weight	Actual Weight	Control Parameters	Maintenance and Adjustments
Signature			Date		Title
Witness			Date		Title

BALANCE CALIBRATION LOG BOOK

Reference:				ID Number:	
Date	Initials	Calibration Weight	Actual Weight	Control Parameters	Maintenance and Adjustments
Signature			Date		Title
Witness			Date		Title

BALANCE CALIBRATION LOG BOOK

Reference: ID Number:

Date	Initials	Calibration Weight	Actual Weight	Control Parameters	Maintenance and Adjustments
Signature			Date		Title
Witness			Date		Title

BALANCE CALIBRATION LOG BOOK

Reference: ID Number:

Date	Initials	Calibration Weight	Actual Weight	Control Parameters	Maintenance and Adjustments
Signature			Date		Title
Witness			Date		Title

BALANCE CALIBRATION LOG BOOK

Reference: ID Number:

Date	Initials	Calibration Weight	Actual Weight	Control Parameters	Maintenance and Adjustments
Signature			Date		Title
Witness			Date		Title

BALANCE CALIBRATION LOG BOOK

Reference: **ID Number:**

Date	Initials	Calibration Weight	Actual Weight	Control Parameters	Maintenance and Adjustments
Signature			Date		Title
Witness			Date		Title

BALANCE CALIBRATION LOG BOOK

Reference:　　　　　　　　　　　　ID Number:

Date	Initials	Calibration Weight	Actual Weight	Control Parameters	Maintenance and Adjustments
Signature			Date		Title
Witness			Date		Title

BALANCE CALIBRATION LOG BOOK

Reference: ID Number:

Date	Initials	Calibration Weight	Actual Weight	Control Parameters	Maintenance and Adjustments
Signature			Date		Title
Witness			Date		Title

BALANCE CALIBRATION LOG BOOK

Reference: ID Number:

Date	Initials	Calibration Weight	Actual Weight	Control Parameters	Maintenance and Adjustments

| Signature | | | Date | | Title | |
| Witness | | | Date | | Title | |

BALANCE CALIBRATION LOG BOOK

Reference: **ID Number:**

Date	Initials	Calibration Weight	Actual Weight	Control Parameters	Maintenance and Adjustments
Signature			Date		Title
Witness			Date		Title

BALANCE CALIBRATION LOG BOOK

Reference: **ID Number:**

Date	Initials	Calibration Weight	Actual Weight	Control Parameters	Maintenance and Adjustments
Signature			Date		Title
Witness			Date		Title

BALANCE CALIBRATION LOG BOOK

Reference:	ID Number:

Date	Initials	Calibration Weight	Actual Weight	Control Parameters	Maintenance and Adjustments
Signature			Date		Title
Witness			Date		Title

BALANCE CALIBRATION LOG BOOK

Reference: **ID Number:**

Date	Initials	Calibration Weight	Actual Weight	Control Parameters	Maintenance and Adjustments
Signature			Date		Title
Witness			Date		Title

BALANCE CALIBRATION LOG BOOK

Reference: **ID Number:**

Date	Initials	Calibration Weight	Actual Weight	Control Parameters	Maintenance and Adjustments

Signature			Date		Title
Witness			Date		Title

BALANCE CALIBRATION LOG BOOK

Reference: **ID Number:**

Date	Initials	Calibration Weight	Actual Weight	Control Parameters	Maintenance and Adjustments
Signature			Date		Title
Witness			Date		Title

BALANCE CALIBRATION LOG BOOK

Reference: ID Number:

Date	Initials	Calibration Weight	Actual Weight	Control Parameters	Maintenance and Adjustments
Signature			Date		Title
Witness			Date		Title

BALANCE CALIBRATION LOG BOOK

Reference: ID Number:

Date	Initials	Calibration Weight	Actual Weight	Control Parameters	Maintenance and Adjustments
Signature			Date		Title
Witness			Date		Title

BALANCE CALIBRATION LOG BOOK

Reference: **ID Number:**

Date	Initials	Calibration Weight	Actual Weight	Control Parameters	Maintenance and Adjustments

| Signature | | | Date | | Title |
| Witness | | | Date | | Title |

BALANCE CALIBRATION LOG BOOK

Reference: **ID Number:**

Date	Initials	Calibration Weight	Actual Weight	Control Parameters	Maintenance and Adjustments
Signature			Date		Title
Witness			Date		Title

BALANCE CALIBRATION LOG BOOK

Reference: ID Number:

Date	Initials	Calibration Weight	Actual Weight	Control Parameters	Maintenance and Adjustments
Signature			Date		Title
Witness			Date		Title

BALANCE CALIBRATION LOG BOOK

Reference: **ID Number:**

Date	Initials	Calibration Weight	Actual Weight	Control Parameters	Maintenance and Adjustments
Signature			Date		Title
Witness			Date		Title

BALANCE CALIBRATION LOG BOOK

Reference: ID Number:

Date	Initials	Calibration Weight	Actual Weight	Control Parameters	Maintenance and Adjustments
Signature			Date		Title
Witness			Date		Title

BALANCE CALIBRATION LOG BOOK

Reference: ID Number:

Date	Initials	Calibration Weight	Actual Weight	Control Parameters	Maintenance and Adjustments
Signature			Date		Title
Witness			Date		Title

BALANCE CALIBRATION LOG BOOK

Reference: ID Number:

Date	Initials	Calibration Weight	Actual Weight	Control Parameters	Maintenance and Adjustments
Signature			Date		Title
Witness			Date		Title

BALANCE CALIBRATION LOG BOOK

Reference: ID Number:

Date	Initials	Calibration Weight	Actual Weight	Control Parameters	Maintenance and Adjustments

| Signature | | Date | | Title | |
| Witness | | Date | | Title | |

BALANCE CALIBRATION LOG BOOK

Reference: **ID Number:**

Date	Initials	Calibration Weight	Actual Weight	Control Parameters	Maintenance and Adjustments

| Signature | | | Date | | Title |
| Witness | | | Date | | Title |

BALANCE CALIBRATION LOG BOOK

Reference: **ID Number:**

Date	Initials	Calibration Weight	Actual Weight	Control Parameters	Maintenance and Adjustments
Signature			Date		Title
Witness			Date		Title

BALANCE CALIBRATION LOG BOOK

Reference: ID Number:

Date	Initials	Calibration Weight	Actual Weight	Control Parameters	Maintenance and Adjustments
Signature			Date		Title
Witness			Date		Title

BALANCE CALIBRATION LOG BOOK

Reference: ID Number:

Date	Initials	Calibration Weight	Actual Weight	Control Parameters	Maintenance and Adjustments
Signature			Date		Title
Witness			Date		Title

BALANCE CALIBRATION LOG BOOK

Reference: ID Number:

Date	Initials	Calibration Weight	Actual Weight	Control Parameters	Maintenance and Adjustments
Signature			Date		Title
Witness			Date		Title

BALANCE CALIBRATION LOG BOOK

Reference: **ID Number:**

Date	Initials	Calibration Weight	Actual Weight	Control Parameters	Maintenance and Adjustments
Signature			Date		Title
Witness			Date		Title

BALANCE CALIBRATION LOG BOOK

Reference: ID Number:

Date	Initials	Calibration Weight	Actual Weight	Control Parameters	Maintenance and Adjustments
Signature			Date		Title	
Witness			Date		Title	

BALANCE CALIBRATION LOG BOOK

Reference: ID Number:

Date	Initials	Calibration Weight	Actual Weight	Control Parameters	Maintenance and Adjustments

Signature		Date		Title	
Witness		Date		Title	

BALANCE CALIBRATION LOG BOOK

Reference: ID Number:

Date	Initials	Calibration Weight	Actual Weight	Control Parameters	Maintenance and Adjustments
Signature			Date		Title
Witness			Date		Title

BALANCE CALIBRATION LOG BOOK

Reference: ID Number:

Date	Initials	Calibration Weight	Actual Weight	Control Parameters	Maintenance and Adjustments
Signature			Date		Title
Witness			Date		Title

BALANCE CALIBRATION LOG BOOK

Reference: ID Number:

Date	Initials	Calibration Weight	Actual Weight	Control Parameters	Maintenance and Adjustments

Signature			Date		Title
Witness			Date		Title

BALANCE CALIBRATION LOG BOOK

Reference: ID Number:

Date	Initials	Calibration Weight	Actual Weight	Control Parameters	Maintenance and Adjustments
Signature			Date		Title
Witness			Date		Title

BALANCE CALIBRATION LOG BOOK

Reference: ID Number:

Date	Initials	Calibration Weight	Actual Weight	Control Parameters	Maintenance and Adjustments

| Signature | | | Date | | Title |
| Witness | | | Date | | Title |

BALANCE CALIBRATION LOG BOOK

Reference: **ID Number:**

Date	Initials	Calibration Weight	Actual Weight	Control Parameters	Maintenance and Adjustments
Signature			Date		Title
Witness			Date		Title

BALANCE CALIBRATION LOG BOOK

Reference: ID Number:

Date	Initials	Calibration Weight	Actual Weight	Control Parameters	Maintenance and Adjustments
Signature			Date		Title
Witness			Date		Title

BALANCE CALIBRATION LOG BOOK

Reference: **ID Number:**

Date	Initials	Calibration Weight	Actual Weight	Control Parameters	Maintenance and Adjustments

Signature		Date		Title	
Witness		Date		Title	

BALANCE CALIBRATION LOG BOOK

Reference: **ID Number:**

Date	Initials	Calibration Weight	Actual Weight	Control Parameters	Maintenance and Adjustments

| Signature | | Date | | Title | |
| Witness | | Date | | Title | |

BALANCE CALIBRATION LOG BOOK

Reference: ID Number:

Date	Initials	Calibration Weight	Actual Weight	Control Parameters	Maintenance and Adjustments
Signature			Date		Title
Witness			Date		Title

BALANCE CALIBRATION LOG BOOK

Reference: ID Number:

Date	Initials	Calibration Weight	Actual Weight	Control Parameters	Maintenance and Adjustments
Signature			Date		Title
Witness			Date		Title

BALANCE CALIBRATION LOG BOOK

Reference: ID Number:

Date	Initials	Calibration Weight	Actual Weight	Control Parameters	Maintenance and Adjustments

Signature		Date		Title	
Witness		Date		Title	

BALANCE CALIBRATION LOG BOOK

Reference: **ID Number:**

Date	Initials	Calibration Weight	Actual Weight	Control Parameters	Maintenance and Adjustments
Signature			Date		Title
Witness			Date		Title

BALANCE CALIBRATION LOG BOOK

Reference: ID Number:

Date	Initials	Calibration Weight	Actual Weight	Control Parameters	Maintenance and Adjustments
Signature			Date		Title
Witness			Date		Title

BALANCE CALIBRATION LOG BOOK

Reference: ID Number:

Date	Initials	Calibration Weight	Actual Weight	Control Parameters	Maintenance and Adjustments
Signature			Date		Title
Witness			Date		Title

BALANCE CALIBRATION LOG BOOK

Reference: ID Number:

Date	Initials	Calibration Weight	Actual Weight	Control Parameters	Maintenance and Adjustments

| Signature | | | Date | | Title |
| Witness | | | Date | | Title |

BALANCE CALIBRATION LOG BOOK

Reference: **ID Number:**

Date	Initials	Calibration Weight	Actual Weight	Control Parameters	Maintenance and Adjustments
Signature			Date		Title
Witness			Date		Title

BALANCE CALIBRATION LOG BOOK

Reference: **ID Number:**

Date	Initials	Calibration Weight	Actual Weight	Control Parameters	Maintenance and Adjustments
Signature			Date		Title
Witness			Date		Title

BALANCE CALIBRATION LOG BOOK

Reference: ID Number:

Date	Initials	Calibration Weight	Actual Weight	Control Parameters	Maintenance and Adjustments
Signature			Date		Title
Witness			Date		Title

BALANCE CALIBRATION LOG BOOK

Reference: **ID Number:**

Date	Initials	Calibration Weight	Actual Weight	Control Parameters	Maintenance and Adjustments
Signature			Date		Title
Witness			Date		Title

BALANCE CALIBRATION LOG BOOK

Reference: **ID Number:**

Date	Initials	Calibration Weight	Actual Weight	Control Parameters	Maintenance and Adjustments
Signature			Date		Title
Witness			Date		Title

BALANCE CALIBRATION LOG BOOK

Reference: **ID Number:**

Date	Initials	Calibration Weight	Actual Weight	Control Parameters	Maintenance and Adjustments
Signature			Date		Title
Witness			Date		Title

BALANCE CALIBRATION LOG BOOK

Reference: ID Number:

Date	Initials	Calibration Weight	Actual Weight	Control Parameters	Maintenance and Adjustments
Signature			Date		Title
Witness			Date		Title

BALANCE CALIBRATION LOG BOOK

Reference: ID Number:

Date	Initials	Calibration Weight	Actual Weight	Control Parameters	Maintenance and Adjustments
Signature			Date		Title
Witness			Date		Title

BALANCE CALIBRATION LOG BOOK

Reference: **ID Number:**

Date	Initials	Calibration Weight	Actual Weight	Control Parameters	Maintenance and Adjustments
Signature			Date		Title
Witness			Date		Title

BALANCE CALIBRATION LOG BOOK

Reference: **ID Number:**

Date	Initials	Calibration Weight	Actual Weight	Control Parameters	Maintenance and Adjustments
Signature			Date		Title
Witness			Date		Title

BALANCE CALIBRATION LOG BOOK

Reference: **ID Number:**

Date	Initials	Calibration Weight	Actual Weight	Control Parameters	Maintenance and Adjustments
Signature			Date		Title
Witness			Date		Title

BALANCE CALIBRATION LOG BOOK

Reference: ID Number:

Date	Initials	Calibration Weight	Actual Weight	Control Parameters	Maintenance and Adjustments
Signature			Date		Title
Witness			Date		Title

BALANCE CALIBRATION LOG BOOK

Reference: **ID Number:**

Date	Initials	Calibration Weight	Actual Weight	Control Parameters	Maintenance and Adjustments
Signature			Date		Title
Witness			Date		Title

BALANCE CALIBRATION LOG BOOK

Reference: **ID Number:**

Date	Initials	Calibration Weight	Actual Weight	Control Parameters	Maintenance and Adjustments
Signature			Date		Title
Witness			Date		Title

BALANCE CALIBRATION LOG BOOK

Reference: ID Number:

Date	Initials	Calibration Weight	Actual Weight	Control Parameters	Maintenance and Adjustments
Signature			Date		Title
Witness			Date		Title

BALANCE CALIBRATION LOG BOOK

Reference: **ID Number:**

Date	Initials	Calibration Weight	Actual Weight	Control Parameters	Maintenance and Adjustments
Signature			Date		Title
Witness			Date		Title

BALANCE CALIBRATION LOG BOOK

Reference: **ID Number:**

Date	Initials	Calibration Weight	Actual Weight	Control Parameters	Maintenance and Adjustments
Signature			Date		Title
Witness			Date		Title

BALANCE CALIBRATION LOG BOOK

Reference: **ID Number:**

Date	Initials	Calibration Weight	Actual Weight	Control Parameters	Maintenance and Adjustments
Signature			Date		Title
Witness			Date		Title

BALANCE CALIBRATION LOG BOOK

Reference: ID Number:

Date	Initials	Calibration Weight	Actual Weight	Control Parameters	Maintenance and Adjustments
Signature			Date		Title
Witness			Date		Title

BALANCE CALIBRATION LOG BOOK

Reference: **ID Number:**

Date	Initials	Calibration Weight	Actual Weight	Control Parameters	Maintenance and Adjustments
Signature			Date		Title
Witness			Date		Title

BALANCE CALIBRATION LOG BOOK

Reference:　　　　　　　　　　　**ID Number:**

Date	Initials	Calibration Weight	Actual Weight	Control Parameters	Maintenance and Adjustments
Signature			Date		Title
Witness			Date		Title

BALANCE CALIBRATION LOG BOOK

Reference: **ID Number:**

Date	Initials	Calibration Weight	Actual Weight	Control Parameters	Maintenance and Adjustments
Signature			Date		Title
Witness			Date		Title

BALANCE CALIBRATION LOG BOOK

Reference: ID Number:

Date	Initials	Calibration Weight	Actual Weight	Control Parameters	Maintenance and Adjustments
Signature				Date		Title
Witness				Date		Title

BALANCE CALIBRATION LOG BOOK

Reference: **ID Number:**

Date	Initials	Calibration Weight	Actual Weight	Control Parameters	Maintenance and Adjustments
Signature			Date		Title
Witness			Date		Title

BALANCE CALIBRATION LOG BOOK

Reference: **ID Number:**

Date	Initials	Calibration Weight	Actual Weight	Control Parameters	Maintenance and Adjustments
Signature			Date		Title
Witness			Date		Title

BALANCE CALIBRATION LOG BOOK

Reference: **ID Number:**

Date	Initials	Calibration Weight	Actual Weight	Control Parameters	Maintenance and Adjustments
Signature			Date		Title
Witness			Date		Title

BALANCE CALIBRATION LOG BOOK

Reference: ID Number:

Date	Initials	Calibration Weight	Actual Weight	Control Parameters	Maintenance and Adjustments
Signature			Date		Title
Witness			Date		Title

BALANCE CALIBRATION LOG BOOK

Reference: ID Number:

Date	Initials	Calibration Weight	Actual Weight	Control Parameters	Maintenance and Adjustments
Signature			Date		Title
Witness			Date		Title

BALANCE CALIBRATION LOG BOOK

Reference: ID Number:

Date	Initials	Calibration Weight	Actual Weight	Control Parameters	Maintenance and Adjustments
Signature			Date		Title
Witness			Date		Title

BALANCE CALIBRATION LOG BOOK

Reference: **ID Number:**

Date	Initials	Calibration Weight	Actual Weight	Control Parameters	Maintenance and Adjustments
Signature			Date		Title
Witness			Date		Title

BALANCE CALIBRATION LOG BOOK

Reference: ID Number:

Date	Initials	Calibration Weight	Actual Weight	Control Parameters	Maintenance and Adjustments
Signature			Date		Title
Witness			Date		Title

BALANCE CALIBRATION LOG BOOK

Reference: ID Number:

Date	Initials	Calibration Weight	Actual Weight	Control Parameters	Maintenance and Adjustments
Signature			Date		Title
Witness			Date		Title

BALANCE CALIBRATION LOG BOOK

Reference: **ID Number:**

Date	Initials	Calibration Weight	Actual Weight	Control Parameters	Maintenance and Adjustments
Signature			Date		Title
Witness			Date		Title

BALANCE CALIBRATION LOG BOOK

Reference: ID Number:

Date	Initials	Calibration Weight	Actual Weight	Control Parameters	Maintenance and Adjustments
Signature			Date		Title
Witness			Date		Title

BALANCE CALIBRATION LOG BOOK

Reference: ID Number:

Date	Initials	Calibration Weight	Actual Weight	Control Parameters	Maintenance and Adjustments
Signature			Date		Title
Witness			Date		Title

BALANCE CALIBRATION LOG BOOK

Reference: **ID Number:**

Date	Initials	Calibration Weight	Actual Weight	Control Parameters	Maintenance and Adjustments
Signature			Date		Title
Witness			Date		Title

BALANCE CALIBRATION LOG BOOK

Reference: **ID Number:**

Date	Initials	Calibration Weight	Actual Weight	Control Parameters	Maintenance and Adjustments
Signature			Date		Title
Witness			Date		Title

BALANCE CALIBRATION LOG BOOK

Reference: **ID Number:**

Date	Initials	Calibration Weight	Actual Weight	Control Parameters	Maintenance and Adjustments
Signature			Date		Title
Witness			Date		Title

BALANCE CALIBRATION LOG BOOK

Reference: ID Number:

Date	Initials	Calibration Weight	Actual Weight	Control Parameters	Maintenance and Adjustments
Signature			Date		Title
Witness			Date		Title

BALANCE CALIBRATION LOG BOOK

Reference: **ID Number:**

Date	Initials	Calibration Weight	Actual Weight	Control Parameters	Maintenance and Adjustments
Signature		Date		Title	
Witness		Date		Title	

BALANCE CALIBRATION LOG BOOK

Reference: ID Number:

Date	Initials	Calibration Weight	Actual Weight	Control Parameters	Maintenance and Adjustments
Signature			Date		Title
Witness			Date		Title

BALANCE CALIBRATION LOG BOOK

Reference: **ID Number:**

Date	Initials	Calibration Weight	Actual Weight	Control Parameters	Maintenance and Adjustments
Signature			Date		Title
Witness			Date		Title

BALANCE CALIBRATION LOG BOOK

Reference: ID Number:

Date	Initials	Calibration Weight	Actual Weight	Control Parameters	Maintenance and Adjustments
Signature			Date		Title
Witness			Date		Title

BALANCE CALIBRATION LOG BOOK

Reference: **ID Number:**

Date	Initials	Calibration Weight	Actual Weight	Control Parameters	Maintenance and Adjustments
Signature			Date		Title
Witness			Date		Title

BALANCE CALIBRATION LOG BOOK

Reference: **ID Number:**

Date	Initials	Calibration Weight	Actual Weight	Control Parameters	Maintenance and Adjustments
Signature			Date		Title
Witness			Date		Title

BALANCE CALIBRATION LOG BOOK

Reference: ID Number:

Date	Initials	Calibration Weight	Actual Weight	Control Parameters	Maintenance and Adjustments
Signature			Date		Title
Witness			Date		Title

BALANCE CALIBRATION LOG BOOK

Reference: ID Number:

Date	Initials	Calibration Weight	Actual Weight	Control Parameters	Maintenance and Adjustments
Signature			Date		Title
Witness			Date		Title

BALANCE CALIBRATION LOG BOOK

Reference: ID Number:

Date	Initials	Calibration Weight	Actual Weight	Control Parameters	Maintenance and Adjustments

| Signature | | Date | | Title | |
| Witness | | Date | | Title | |

BALANCE CALIBRATION LOG BOOK

Reference: **ID Number:**

Date	Initials	Calibration Weight	Actual Weight	Control Parameters	Maintenance and Adjustments
Signature			Date		Title
Witness			Date		Title

BALANCE CALIBRATION LOG BOOK

Reference: **ID Number:**

Date	Initials	Calibration Weight	Actual Weight	Control Parameters	Maintenance and Adjustments
Signature			Date		Title
Witness			Date		Title

BALANCE CALIBRATION LOG BOOK

Reference: ID Number:

Date	Initials	Calibration Weight	Actual Weight	Control Parameters	Maintenance and Adjustments
Signature			Date		Title
Witness			Date		Title

BALANCE CALIBRATION LOG BOOK

Reference: ID Number:

Date	Initials	Calibration Weight	Actual Weight	Control Parameters	Maintenance and Adjustments
Signature			Date		Title
Witness			Date		Title

BALANCE CALIBRATION LOG BOOK

Reference:				ID Number:	
Date	Initials	Calibration Weight	Actual Weight	Control Parameters	Maintenance and Adjustments
Signature			Date		Title
Witness			Date		Title

BALANCE CALIBRATION LOG BOOK

Reference: **ID Number:**

Date	Initials	Calibration Weight	Actual Weight	Control Parameters	Maintenance and Adjustments
Signature			Date		Title
Witness			Date		Title

BALANCE CALIBRATION LOG BOOK

Reference: ID Number:

Date	Initials	Calibration Weight	Actual Weight	Control Parameters	Maintenance and Adjustments
Signature			Date		Title
Witness			Date		Title

BALANCE CALIBRATION LOG BOOK

Reference: ID Number:

Date	Initials	Calibration Weight	Actual Weight	Control Parameters	Maintenance and Adjustments

| Signature | | | Date | | Title |
| Witness | | | Date | | Title |

BALANCE CALIBRATION LOG BOOK

Reference: ID Number:

Date	Initials	Calibration Weight	Actual Weight	Control Parameters	Maintenance and Adjustments
Signature			Date		Title
Witness			Date		Title

BALANCE CALIBRATION LOG BOOK

Reference: **ID Number:**

Date	Initials	Calibration Weight	Actual Weight	Control Parameters	Maintenance and Adjustments
Signature			Date		Title
Witness			Date		Title

BALANCE CALIBRATION LOG BOOK

Reference: ID Number:

Date	Initials	Calibration Weight	Actual Weight	Control Parameters	Maintenance and Adjustments
Signature			Date		Title
Witness			Date		Title

BALANCE CALIBRATION LOG BOOK

Reference: **ID Number:**

Date	Initials	Calibration Weight	Actual Weight	Control Parameters	Maintenance and Adjustments
Signature			Date		Title
Witness			Date		Title

BALANCE CALIBRATION LOG BOOK

Reference: **ID Number:**

Date	Initials	Calibration Weight	Actual Weight	Control Parameters	Maintenance and Adjustments
Signature			Date		Title
Witness			Date		Title

BALANCE CALIBRATION LOG BOOK

Reference: **ID Number:**

Date	Initials	Calibration Weight	Actual Weight	Control Parameters	Maintenance and Adjustments
Signature			Date		Title
Witness			Date		Title

BALANCE CALIBRATION LOG BOOK

Reference: ID Number:

Date	Initials	Calibration Weight	Actual Weight	Control Parameters	Maintenance and Adjustments

| Signature | | Date | | Title | |
| Witness | | Date | | Title | |

BALANCE CALIBRATION LOG BOOK

Reference: ID Number:

Date	Initials	Calibration Weight	Actual Weight	Control Parameters	Maintenance and Adjustments
Signature			Date		Title
Witness			Date		Title

BALANCE CALIBRATION LOG BOOK

Reference: ID Number:

Date	Initials	Calibration Weight	Actual Weight	Control Parameters	Maintenance and Adjustments
Signature			Date		Title
Witness			Date		Title

BALANCE CALIBRATION LOG BOOK

Reference: **ID Number:**

Date	Initials	Calibration Weight	Actual Weight	Control Parameters	Maintenance and Adjustments
Signature			Date		Title
Witness			Date		Title

BALANCE CALIBRATION LOG BOOK

Reference: ID Number:

Date	Initials	Calibration Weight	Actual Weight	Control Parameters	Maintenance and Adjustments
Signature			Date		Title
Witness			Date		Title

BALANCE CALIBRATION LOG BOOK

Reference: **ID Number:**

Date	Initials	Calibration Weight	Actual Weight	Control Parameters	Maintenance and Adjustments
Signature			Date		Title
Witness			Date		Title

BALANCE CALIBRATION LOG BOOK

Reference: **ID Number:**

Date	Initials	Calibration Weight	Actual Weight	Control Parameters	Maintenance and Adjustments

| Signature | | | Date | | Title |
| Witness | | | Date | | Title |

BALANCE CALIBRATION LOG BOOK

Reference: **ID Number:**

Date	Initials	Calibration Weight	Actual Weight	Control Parameters	Maintenance and Adjustments
Signature			Date		Title
Witness			Date		Title

BALANCE CALIBRATION LOG BOOK

Reference: ID Number:

Date	Initials	Calibration Weight	Actual Weight	Control Parameters	Maintenance and Adjustments
Signature			Date		Title
Witness			Date		Title

BALANCE CALIBRATION LOG BOOK

Reference: ID Number:

Date	Initials	Calibration Weight	Actual Weight	Control Parameters	Maintenance and Adjustments
Signature			Date		Title
Witness			Date		Title

BALANCE CALIBRATION LOG BOOK

Reference:				ID Number:	
Date	Initials	Calibration Weight	Actual Weight	Control Parameters	Maintenance and Adjustments
Signature			Date		Title
Witness			Date		Title

BALANCE CALIBRATION LOG BOOK

Reference: **ID Number:**

Date	Initials	Calibration Weight	Actual Weight	Control Parameters	Maintenance and Adjustments
Signature			Date		Title
Witness			Date		Title

BALANCE CALIBRATION LOG BOOK

Reference: ID Number:

Date	Initials	Calibration Weight	Actual Weight	Control Parameters	Maintenance and Adjustments
Signature			Date		Title
Witness			Date		Title

BALANCE CALIBRATION LOG BOOK

Reference: ID Number:

Date	Initials	Calibration Weight	Actual Weight	Control Parameters	Maintenance and Adjustments

Signature			Date		Title
Witness			Date		Title

BALANCE CALIBRATION LOG BOOK

Reference: ID Number:

Date	Initials	Calibration Weight	Actual Weight	Control Parameters	Maintenance and Adjustments

| Signature | | | Date | | Title |
| Witness | | | Date | | Title |

BALANCE CALIBRATION LOG BOOK

Reference: **ID Number:**

Date	Initials	Calibration Weight	Actual Weight	Control Parameters	Maintenance and Adjustments
Signature			Date		Title
Witness			Date		Title

BALANCE CALIBRATION LOG BOOK

Reference: ID Number:

Date	Initials	Calibration Weight	Actual Weight	Control Parameters	Maintenance and Adjustments
Signature			Date		Title
Witness			Date		Title

BALANCE CALIBRATION LOG BOOK

Reference: ID Number:

Date	Initials	Calibration Weight	Actual Weight	Control Parameters	Maintenance and Adjustments
Signature			Date		Title
Witness			Date		Title

BALANCE CALIBRATION LOG BOOK

Reference: **ID Number:**

Date	Initials	Calibration Weight	Actual Weight	Control Parameters	Maintenance and Adjustments
Signature			Date		Title
Witness			Date		Title

BALANCE CALIBRATION LOG BOOK

Reference: **ID Number:**

Date	Initials	Calibration Weight	Actual Weight	Control Parameters	Maintenance and Adjustments

| Signature | | | Date | | Title |
| Witness | | | Date | | Title |

BALANCE CALIBRATION LOG BOOK

Reference: ID Number:

Date	Initials	Calibration Weight	Actual Weight	Control Parameters	Maintenance and Adjustments
Signature			Date		Title
Witness			Date		Title

BALANCE CALIBRATION LOG BOOK

Reference: **ID Number:**

Date	Initials	Calibration Weight	Actual Weight	Control Parameters	Maintenance and Adjustments
Signature			Date		Title
Witness			Date		Title

BALANCE CALIBRATION LOG BOOK

Reference: **ID Number:**

Date	Initials	Calibration Weight	Actual Weight	Control Parameters	Maintenance and Adjustments
Signature			Date		Title
Witness			Date		Title

BALANCE CALIBRATION LOG BOOK

Reference: ID Number:

Date	Initials	Calibration Weight	Actual Weight	Control Parameters	Maintenance and Adjustments
Signature			Date		Title
Witness			Date		Title

BALANCE CALIBRATION LOG BOOK

Reference: ID Number:

Date	Initials	Calibration Weight	Actual Weight	Control Parameters	Maintenance and Adjustments
Signature			Date		Title
Witness			Date		Title

BALANCE CALIBRATION LOG BOOK

Reference: **ID Number:**

Date	Initials	Calibration Weight	Actual Weight	Control Parameters	Maintenance and Adjustments

| Signature | | | Date | | Title |
| Witness | | | Date | | Title |

BALANCE CALIBRATION LOG BOOK

Reference: **ID Number:**

Date	Initials	Calibration Weight	Actual Weight	Control Parameters	Maintenance and Adjustments
Signature			Date		Title
Witness			Date		Title

BALANCE CALIBRATION LOG BOOK

Reference: **ID Number:**

Date	Initials	Calibration Weight	Actual Weight	Control Parameters	Maintenance and Adjustments

| Signature | | | Date | | Title |
| Witness | | | Date | | Title |

BALANCE CALIBRATION LOG BOOK

Reference: ID Number:

Date	Initials	Calibration Weight	Actual Weight	Control Parameters	Maintenance and Adjustments

| Signature | | | Date | | Title |
| Witness | | | Date | | Title |

BALANCE CALIBRATION LOG BOOK

Reference: ID Number:

Date	Initials	Calibration Weight	Actual Weight	Control Parameters	Maintenance and Adjustments
Signature			Date		Title
Witness			Date		Title

BALANCE CALIBRATION LOG BOOK

Reference: **ID Number:**

Date	Initials	Calibration Weight	Actual Weight	Control Parameters	Maintenance and Adjustments
Signature			Date		Title
Witness			Date		Title

BALANCE CALIBRATION LOG BOOK

Reference: ID Number:

Date	Initials	Calibration Weight	Actual Weight	Control Parameters	Maintenance and Adjustments
Signature			Date		Title
Witness			Date		Title

www.ingramcontent.com/pod-product-compliance
Lightning Source LLC
Chambersburg PA
CBHW081606200526
45169CB00021B/2128